All About Canada

100+ Fascinating Fun Facts & Trivia

By Bandana Ojha

Introduction

Filled with up-to-date information, color photos, fascinating & fun facts this book " All About Canada: 100+ Fascinating Fun Facts & Trivia" is the best book for kids as well the entire family to find out more about Canada. This book would satisfy the children's curiosity and help them to understand why Canada is special—and what makes it different from other country. This book gives a story, history, the official symbols, how Canada got its name, people, places and many more. It is a fun way for young readers to find out more interesting and fun facts of the world's the best-educated country. This is a great chance for every kid as well as the entire family to expand their knowledge about one of and wealthiest nation and impress their friends with all "discovered and never knew before" amazing and interesting fun facts.

1. Canada is the second largest country in the world in area after Russia.

2. Canada occupies much of the continent of North America, sharing land borders with the contiguous United States to the south and the U.S. state of Alaska to the northwest.

3.Canada shares the longest land border in the world with the United States, totaling 5525 miles.

4.Canada stretches from the Atlantic Ocean in the east to the Pacific Ocean in the west, Arctic Ocean to the north.

5. Canada features the longest coastline in the world, stretching 125570 miles.

6. Prior to European colonization, the present-day Canada were inhabited for millennia by Indigenous peoples.

7. John Cabot was the first explorer to reach Canada in 1497.

8. Starting in the late 15th century, French and British expeditions explored, colonized, and fought over various places within North America in what constitutes present-day Canada.

9. The name "Canada" likely comes from the word "kanata," meaning "village" or "settlement." In 1535, two Aboriginal youths told French explorer Jacques Cartier about the route to kanata; they were referring to the village of Stadacona, the site of the present-day City of Québec. Cartier used the word "Canada" to describe not only the village, but the entire area controlled by its chief, Donnacona.

10. The first use of Canada as an official name came in 1791, when the Province of Quebec was divided into the colonies of Upper Canada and Lower Canada. In 1841,

the two colonies were united under one name, the Province of Canada.

11. Canada came into being as a country on July 1, 1867 when the British Parliament passed the British North America Act.

12. July 1st is celebrated as Canada Day and Canadians set off fireworks, drink beer and wear festive red and white clothing.

13. Canada became its own independent country in 1982.

14. Ottawa is the capital city of Canada.

15. It stands on the south bank of the Ottawa River in the eastern portion of southern Ontario.

16. It is the second coldest capital in the world after Moscow.

17. The flag of Canada is the official national flag of Canada.

18. It consists of a red field with a white square at its center in the ratio of 1:2:1, in the middle of which is featured a stylized, red, 11-pointed maple leaf charged in the center.

19. It is the first flag to have been adopted by both houses of Parliament and officially proclaimed by the Canadian monarch as the country's official national flag.

20. The national anthem of Canada is "O Canada".

21. The original lyrics were in French; an English translation was published in 1906.

22. The French lyrics remain unaltered. "O Canada" officially becoming the country's national anthem in 1980 when Canada's National Anthem Act received royal assent and became effective on July 1 as part of that year's Canada Day celebrations.

23."God Save the Queen" is the royal anthem of Canada.

24. The Great Seal of Canada is a governmental seal used for purposes of state in Canada, being set on letters patent, proclamations and commissions, both to representatives of the Queen and for the appointment of cabinet ministers, senators, and judges.

25. Many other officials, such as officers in the Canadian Armed Forces, receive commissions affixed with the Privy Seal, not the great seal. Although not an official symbol of Canada the seal is one of the

oldest and most honored instruments of the Canadian government.

26. "A Mari Usque Ad Mare" is the Canadian national motto.

27. The motto was first officially used in 1906 on the head of the mace of the new Legislative Assembly of Saskatchewan.

28. Red and white are the national colors of Canada.

29. National colors were declared by King George V in 1921 and are most prominently evident on the country's national flag.

30. The maple tree was officially proclaimed national arboreal emblem of Canada on 25th April 1996.

31. The maple tree is the national tree of Canada.

32. Canada has two national animals, the beaver, and the Canadian Horse.

33. The beaver is the national animal of Canada since 1975.

35. The government of Canada passed a bill in 2002, which made the Canadian Horse an official symbol and a national animal of Canada.

36. Canada's beaver is the second largest rodent in the world, weighing up to 60 pounds.

37. The largest rodent is the capybara, found in South America and weighing up to 100 pounds.

38. There is no official bird of Canada.

39. There are about 630 bird species in Canada.

40. Ice hockey and Lacrosse are two official sports of Canada.

41. Ice hockey is declared to be the national winter sport of Canada and Lacrosse is

declared to be the national summer sport of Canada.

42. The first indoor ice hockey game took place on March 3, 1875 at the Victoria Skating Rink in Montreal.

43. The Royal Montreal Golf Club, founded in 1873, is the oldest golf club in North America.

44. The Maple Leaf Tartan is used by The Royal Canadian Regiment Pipes and Drums, and has also been worn by the 2nd, 3rd, and 4th Battalions.

45. The Maple Leaf Tartan was declared an official national symbol on March 9, 2011.

46. A symbol of national pride, the tartan was designed to be worn by Canadians from all backgrounds regardless of their ancestry on national days like Canada Day and Tartan Day.

47. A developed country, Canada has the seventeenth-highest nominal per-capita income globally as well as the thirteenth-highest ranking in the Human Development Index.

48. Canada is the world's tenth-largest economy as of 2018, with a nominal GDP of approximately US$1.73 trillion.

49. It is one of the least corrupt countries in the world and is one of the world's top ten trading nations, with a highly globalized economy.

50. The Toronto Stock Exchange is the ninth-largest stock exchange in the world by market capitalization, listing over 1,500 companies with a combined market capitalization of over US$2 trillion.

51. Contributing to its title as the world's most educated country, the literacy rate in Canada is 99%.

52. There have been 10 Nobel Prize laureates in Canada.

53. French and English are the two official languages in Canada.

54. Canadians used a mix of American and British English when writing.

55. Canada is made up of 10 provinces and 3 territories.

56. Toronto, Montreal, Vancouver, Edmonton, and Calgary are major cities of Canada.

57. The biggest city in Canada is Toronto.

58. Quebec is the country's largest province with a total land area of 1.5 million sq. km.

59. Prince Edward Island is the smallest province with a total land area of at 5,660 sq. km.

60. Among the territories, Nunavut is the largest, taking up one-fifth of Canada's total land area (2 million sq.km).

61. Despite having all this space, Nunavut is home to only about 38,000 people because of its harsh climate and remoteness.

62. Fifty percent of the world's polar bears live in Nunavut.

63. The license plate for cars, motorbikes and snowmobiles in Nunavut is in the shape of a polar bear.

64. Canada ranks third in oil reserves only after Saudi Arabia and Venezuela.

65. Canada is home to approximately 60% of the world's polar bear population.

66. Despite being a huge country, Canada has the fourth lowest population density in the world, with only three people living per square km.

67. Basketball was invented by a Canadian whose name was Dr. James Naismith. He

invented the game with a group of college students in Boston.

68. The baseball glove was invented in Canada in 1883.

69. The first indoor hockey game took place in Montreal on March 3, 1875.

70. Montreal, Canada's second biggest city after Toronto, is the second biggest city in the world that has a French-speaking population after Paris.

71. 77% of the maple syrup in the world is made in Quebec, Canada.

72. Canada has more doughnut shops per capita than any other country in the world.

73. The highest point of Canada is Mount Logan, Yukon Territory.

74. It is 5959 meters (19,551 feet) high.

75. The lowest point of Canada is Great Slave Lake Bottom, Northwest Territories.

76. The coldest temperature ever recorded in Canada was -63°C on February 3, 1957 in Snag, Yukon.

77. The coldest wind-chill ever recorded in Canada was in Pelly Bay, Northwest Territories and was -91 Celsius (-131.8 Fahrenheit) in 1989.

78. Ocean Falls, British Columbia has on average 330 days of rain per year.

79. Estevan, Saskatchewan is the sunniest place in Canada.

80. The total population of Canada is estimated as 37.59 million (2019).

81. 81 percent of the total population resides in cities.

82. About 90% of Canada's population is concentrated within 100 miles of the Canada/US border.

83. Manitoba was the first province to grant women the right to vote.

84 Nearly 22% of Canada's population is immigrants.

85. Canada is the largest producer of uranium in the world.

86. Canada is second biggest producer of hydroelectric power - after China.

87. Canada is the number 1 donut consumer in the world. People in Canada consume 1-billion donuts annually.

88. In Churchill Manitoba, nobody locks their doors to their house or cars in case of a polar bear attack.

89. Wasaga Beach in Ontario is the longest freshwater beach in the world.

90. Three of the largest islands in the world are located within Canada – Baffin Island, Victoria Island, and Ellesmere Island.

91. Canada has more lakes than the rest of the world combined. There may be as many as millions, with 563 of them larger than 100 square kilometers.

92. Among all largest lakes are Lake Huron in Ontario, Great Bear Lake in the Northwestern Territories and Lake Superior in Ontario.

93. Despite being larger in area than the United States, Canada has just about 11% of the population of that found in the U.S.

94. Canadians, just like Americans, celebrate Thanksgiving on the second Monday in October.

95. There are 42 national parks and 167 national historic sites located in Canada.

96. Canada has six time zones.

97. The Trans-Canada highway is said to be the longest national highway in the world.

98. Canadians eat more Mac and Cheese than anyone else in the world.

99. Cheddar is the most popular cheese in Canada. On average Canadians consume 23.4 pounds per person annually.

100. Canadians drink more fruit juice per capita than any other country.

101. There are more doughnut shops in Canada per capita than any other country.

101. IMAX was invented by Graeme Ferguson, Roman Kroitor and Robert Kerr in 1967. Three Canadian filmmakers.

102. Insulin was discovered by Doctor Frederick Banting in 19921 at the University of Toronto.

103. There are about 200 species of mammals in Canada.

104. There are nearly 2.5 million caribou in Canada.

105. Canada was ranked the number -1 destination to visit in the world in 2017 by "The New York Times".

106. "Hawaiian" pizza was invented by an Ontario man, not by the Hawaiians.

106. The Canadian/US border is the longest border in the world that lacks military defense.

108. Kim Campbell was Canada's first (and only) female Prime Minister.

109. The Château Frontenac in Quebec City is said to be the most photographed hotel in the world.

110. Up to 30% of Canada is covered in trees and thick forest.

111. Quebec City, Quebec is the only walled city north of Mexico.

112. The longest bridge in Canada is Confederation Bridge. It is almost 13 kilometers long and transports about 4,000 vehicles each day.

Please check this out:

Our other best-selling books for kids are-

All About **New York:** 100+ Amazing Facts with Pictures

All About **New Jersey**: 100+ Amazing Facts with Pictures

All About **California:** 100+ Amazing Facts with Pictures

All About **Arizona**: 100+ Amazing Facts with Pictures

All About **Massachusetts**: 100+ Amazing Facts with Pictures

All About **Minnesota:** 100+ Amazing Facts with Pictures

All About **Florida**: 100+ Amazing Facts with Pictures

All About **Texas:** 100+ Amazing Facts with Pictures

All About **Italy**: 100+ Amazing Facts with Pictures

All About **Australia**: 100+ Amazing Facts with Pictures

Know about **Sharks**: 100 Amazing Fun Facts with Pictures

Know About **Whales**:100+ Amazing & Interesting Fun Facts with Pictures

Know About **Dinosaurs**: 100 Amazing & Interesting Fun Facts with Pictures

Know About **Kangaroos**: Amazing & Interesting Facts with Pictures

Know About **Penguins**: 100+ Amazing Penguin Facts with Pictures

Know About **Dolphins** :100 Amazing Dolphin Facts with Pictures

Know About **Elephant**

Most Popular Animal Quiz book for Kids: 100 amazing animal facts

Quiz Book for Kids: Science, History, Geography, Biology, Computer & Information Technology

English Grammar for Kids: Most Easy Way to learn English Grammar

Solar System & Space Science- Quiz for Kids: What You Know About Solar System

100 Amazing Quiz Q & A About Penguin: Never Known Before Penguin Facts

English Grammar Practice Book for elementary kids: 1000+ Practice Questions with Answers

A to Z of English Tense

My First Fruits

* 9 7 9 8 6 6 3 6 9 7 6 6 8 *